Silly Nomads

Volume 1 Teacher's Guide

Silly Nomads From Palmerston Close

Written in collaboration with Progressive Bridges, Inc.
©2017 Mohalland Lewis LLC

© 2017 Mohalland Lewis, LLC
All rights reserved.

© 2015 Document Text
Written in collaboration with
Progressive Bridges, Inc., Naples, FL

Published in the United States by
Mohalland Lewis, LLC

Cover Illustration by Kate Santee

No part of this book may be reproduced, scanned, stored in a retrieval system, or transmitted by any means without the written permission of Mohalland Lewis, LLC.

ISBN 978-0-9990303-0-1

This lesson plan is suitable for use with students in Grades 3-5. All activities are aligned with the ELA Common Core State Standards (CCSS) for Reading, Writing, and Speaking & Listening. Activities can be modified as needed based on specific needs and ability levels within those standards.

Learning Objectives:

1. Identify characteristics of nomadic desert life.
2. Explain and give examples of real and imaginary story events.
3. Compare and contrast characters and settings with one's own life experiences.
4. Engage in using the imagination to create new adventures and expand ideas and possibilities.
5. Utilize and grow literacy skills through story interaction.

This story supports the following beliefs:

- Education is valuable to personal success in life.
- New knowledge can fuel imagination.
- Using your imagination is a fun, inexpensive, and powerful experience.
- Entertainment and happiness can be found without a lot of material possessions.

Note to the Teacher:

Use this lesson plan as a flexible guide to support **Silly Nomads – Volume 1** with a variety of options from which to choose based on your students' interests and ability levels. All activities are aligned with the ELA Common Core State Standards (CCSS) to ensure quality, relevance, and rigor in the academic classroom. Best practice pages for instructional vocabulary activities and read-a-loud strategies are listed on pages 31-33 of this lesson plan document.

A Lesson Guide for Teachers

- **This lesson plan** provides educators with several activity menus that include a range of specific reading skill activities and open-ended questions, aligned with Common Core State Standards (CCSS), enabling students to create meaningful connections to story characters and events as they enhance critical thinking, reading, writing, speaking, and listening skills.

- **This lesson plan** provides educators with cross-curriculum activities to reinforce concepts in social studies, geography, math, science, and the arts, as well as in the area of literacy. Look for specific icons for these connections.

- **This lesson plan** provides educators with a menu of engaging activities for elementary students designed to help them extend their learning by encouraging imaginative and innovative ideas, much like the story characters. Many activities also involve research-related skills designed to appeal to 21st Century learners as they explore a variety of concepts and possible career interests. These activities can be easily modified or adapted for children of many ages, maturity levels, and academic ability levels.

A Home Connection for Students and Parents

- **This lesson plan** provides teachers with learning activities and discussion prompts for students to share with their parents at home to reinforce learning concepts, promote literacy in families, and to provide ways to keep parents connected to the classroom.

 Home Connection Activity

Assessments to Check for Understanding

- **This lesson plan** provides teachers with several assessments to measure student understanding of the story. A Pre and Post Assessment given at the beginning and end of the book provide evidence of concept learning throughout the story. A short 10 question quiz is part of every lesson and measures student comprehension of the part of the book covered for that specific lesson. While most questions are multiple choice or true/false, quizzes do contain a few open-ended responses. A final Reading Comprehension Assessment provides an open-ended response assessment to measure further story comprehension.

Silly Nomads From Palmerston Close

Lesson #1   Chapters 1-3   Pages 1-34

Lesson Focus - Introduction of the Nomads which are the main characters (Suhcrom and Naddih) and their friends through a crab catching adventure. Suhcrom and Naddih become nomads and start their adventure.

Basic Story Vocabulary   (2-5, Reading – Standard 4)

anticipation	nomads	freedom	scurried
cardboard	oasis	promised	mischievous
crouched	proclaimed	fascinating	suspicious
discarded	residential	imitating	sheepishly
documentary	scheming	rambled	established

Pre-teach vocabulary to introduce students to new words prior to reading the chapter. Choose an *Instructional Vocabulary Activity* from page 31.

Reading the Text

Silly Nomads books make fun read-aloud experiences for students. Varying these strategies reinforces interaction with text and creates ongoing interest for students. Choose a *Read-Aloud Strategy* from page 32-33 for in-class reading.

Facilitated Discussion Prompts

Discuss in pairs for 2-3 minutes what the boys think about right before they go on their adventure. (2-5, Speaking & Listening – Standards 1, 2, & 6)

Discuss with a group what kinds of things you would take on an adventure if you could only take (3) things. (2-5, Speaking & Listening – Standards 1, 2, & 6)

👀 Predict, discuss and make a strong inference about what will happen in the next reading selection. Base your answer on what happened in today's passage. (2-5, Speaking & Listening – Standards 1, 2, & 6)

👀 Listen to a short 1 to 2 minute YouTube audio presentation about an adventure. Compare and contrast this adventure and the adventure of Silly Nomads so far. (2-5, Speaking & Listening – Standards 1, 2, & 6)

👀 With a partner, tell a 2-3 minute story about an adventure that you took. Describe who was with you, where you went, what you did. (2-5, Speaking & Listening – Standards 1, 2, & 6)

Reading Comprehension Activities

👀 Create a timeline of words and pictures to retell 5 – 10 events of the story in the order in which they occurred. Add to your story map as you continue to read the book. (2-5, Reading – Standard 2)

👀 Describe the characters in the story using a cartoon bubble with words and phrases coming out of their mouth as they respond to major events and challenges they encounter. (2-5, Reading – Standards 1, 2, & 4)

👀 Identify new words that the characters say in the story that appeal to the five senses. Draw a model of eye, ear, and mouth and explain how the new words look and sound according to the five senses. (2-5, Reading – Standards 1, 2, & 4)

👀 Pick out the conversation quotes written in the text and explain what they mean. (2-5, Reading – Standards 1, 2, & 4)

👀 Create an interactive vocabulary list and game using Kahoot (www.Kahoot.com) and share it with the class. (2-5, Reading – Standard 4)

👀 Create a Venn Diagram comparing and contrasting the two characters in the story. Use words or pictures to describe how they are different and alike. (2-5, Reading – Standards 1 & 2)

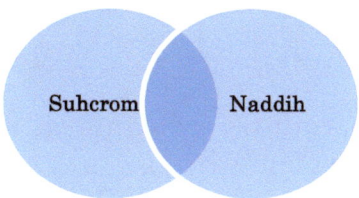

Writing Prompts

👀 💡 Imagine that you are going on an adventure with your friends- where would you go? What would you do? What friends would you tell and bring with you? Write a story about the adventure. Publish the story and share it with the class. (2-5, Writing – Standards 3, 5, & 6)

👀 💡 Create and share a five slide PowerPoint describing the main characters in Silly Nomads. (2-5, Writing – Standard 1)

👀 💡 Use the language in the book to create your own language to express the feelings of the main characters as they catch the crab. Write 3-4 lines of your new language to share. (2-5, Writing – Standard 1; 2-5, Speaking & Listening – Standard 1, 2, & 6)

👀 🎨 Draw and write a 5 page diary about the boys adventures when catching the crab. (2-5, Writing – Standard 1)

 Create a conversation between the two characters based on what you know of their personalities and mannerisms. Be sure to punctuate the dialogue correctly with quotation marks and periods in the correct locations.   (2-5, Writing – Standard 2)

Curriculum Connections

 Discover Jamaica

Watch a video clip to discover the country of Jamaica and the neighborhood of Palmerston Close, in the city of Portsmouth. Use a Venn Diagram to list three similarities and differences between the United States and Jamaica.   (2-5, Reading – Standards 1 & 2)

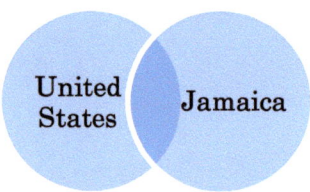

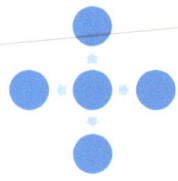 Crab Tasting

Discover what elements are in a scotch bonnet pepper and why it would taste good with crab that the boys caught. Describe the taste based on your research by creating a bubble map of descriptive words. Then, create your own crab recipe. Type it up on a recipe card and try to make it with a parent.   (2-5, Reading – Standards 1, 2, and 6)

 **3-D Figure**

Create a 3-D figure symbolizing something from the story that you read so far. (2-5, Reading – Standards 1 & 2)

 **Travel Brochure**

Find pictures in an old magazine and make an imaginative collage for a travel brochure to a new place you create. Use information from the internet to add to your collage. Add the location name and descriptive words throughout the brochure to entice others to travel there. (2-5, Reading – Standards 1 & 2)

 **Plotting an Adventure**

Research and develop a timeline plotting seven points of travel in a Nomad Adventure beginning in Palmerston Close-Jamaica and ending in another Jamaican city. Use the timeline to extend your adventure to power point describing events you encountered along the way. (2-5, Reading – Standards 1 & 2)

 **Buddy Book**

Create a buddy book to share with your friends about "If you could go anywhere, where would you go and who would you take with you? (2-5, Reading – Standards 1 & 2)

Research & Imagination Activities

 **Imagine Dragons…**

Imagine facing dragons, snakes, and wolves that came out of the hole when the boys were chasing the crab. Draw and color each animal coming out of the hole before the crab. Tell how the boys feel when seeing this by creating captions for the pictures. (2-5, Writing – Standards 2, 6, 7, & 8; 2-5, Reading – Standard 9)

 **Imagine Being a Nomad...**

Imagine you are a Nomad. Use a shoebox to create a tent where you will stay when you are on your adventure. Include in the shoebox (5) items that you will take with you on your adventure. Write about your tent and the items that you will take with you on your adventure on 3- 5 index cards. Present your adventure preparation with your shoebox and index cards to your class. (2-5, Writing – Standards 2, 7, & 8)

 **Imagine Jamaica...**

Imagine living in Jamaica. Research more about the country and their culture. Design and create a placemat of real adventures in Jamaica based on your findings. (2-5, Writing – Standards 2, 7, & 8; 2-5, Reading – Standard 9)

 **Crab Catching Flowchart**

Imagine that you are called upon to give crab catching lessons. Research the art of crab catching beyond what you know of the boys' experiences. Create a flowchart t show each step of this process. Be creative with your visual presentation of the flowchart. (2-5, Writing – Standards 2, 7, & 8; 2-5, Reading – Standard 9)

Silly Nomads From Palmerston Close - Volume 1

Lesson #1   Home Connection Activities

🏠 Find a towel at your home to make a secret nomad hat. Take this new hat on a secret adventure. Keep a weeks diary about the adventures that you go on and who you invite to go with you.

🏠 List characters in the story that you read about. Create two new characters in the story selection that are round characters. Round characters are fully described and it is clear as to why they are included in the story selection. Draw and share your round characters with your parents and teacher.

🏠 Find a small box at home and find pictures from Jamaica on the internet. Draw or print four pictures to decorate your box. Use this box to collect different items after you read each section of the book. Share what you have in your box with your parents after each reading lessson and then at the end of the book. Be sure to explain what the item is , why you put it in your box, and how it relates to the story.

🏠 Make a clay clay model of the nomads going on an an adventure. Include items that they collect on their adventure and display this in an open shoebox. Make the shoebox into a stage to share the story with others.

WE CONNECTED!

My favorite character in this part of the story was _____

because he/she _____

I liked the part in the story when _____

_____

I circled the house beside of the activity we completed.

Student: _____   Date: _____

Parent(s): _____   Date: _____

This page may be copied for student/parent use.

Silly Nomads From Palmerston Close

Lesson #2   Chapters 4-6   Pages 35-67

Lesson Focus: Suhcrom and Naddih continue their adventure in the desert. They discover bones, discover the meaning of proper preparation, and set up a tent.

Basic Story Vocabulary   (2-5, Reading – Standard 4)

overwhelming	destination	turbans	folklore
sprawled	malaria	resourceful	omniscient
meandered	recounting	wander	ration
inevitable	quenched	snatched	gangrene
stifle	glint	gibberish	shrouded

Pre-teach vocabulary to introduce students to new words prior to reading the chapter. Choose an *Instructional Vocabulary Activity* from page 31.

Reading the Text

Silly Nomads books make fun read-aloud experiences for students. Varying these strategies reinforces interaction with text and creates ongoing interest for students. Choose a *Read-Aloud Strategy* from page 32-33 for in-class reading.

Facilitated Discussion Prompts

👀 Discuss in pairs for 2-3 minutes what the boys found lying in a clump of weeds. (2-5, Speaking & Listening – Standards 1, 2, & 6)

👀 Discuss with a group who or what you think the skeleton that the boys found belonged to. Support your answer. (2-5, Speaking & Listening – Standards 1, 2, & 6)

👀 Predict, discuss, and make a strong inference about whether or not you think the bones-skeleton was the blind dog that everyone talked about. Support your

15

answer from information provided in the text. (2-5, Speaking & Listening – Standards 1, 2, & 6)

👓 With a partner, make the sounds that Suhcrom used when retelling the story of the blind dog, Helmet - BANG-BAM-NOOO-ROARRRR. (2-5, Speaking & Listening – Standards 1, 2, & 6)

👓 With a partner, play a 3-4 minute game using a blindfold to see and feel what it may be like to be blind. Your partner can guide you through a maze of two feet with books, juice boxes, and shoes to step over. (2-5, Speaking & Listening – Standards 1, 2, & 6)

Reading Comprehension Activities

👓 Create a timeline of words and pictures to retell 5 – 10 events of the story in the order in which they occurred starting at 10 o'clock AM and ending when Suhcrom and Naddih make it across the desert to the top of the hill. Add to your story map as you continue to read the book from the top of the hill until the boys finally return home. (2-5, Reading – Standard 2)

👓 Describe the characters in the story using a cartoon bubble with words and phrases coming out of their mouths as they respond to the idea of using Jomfeh's knife in their adventure.
(2-5, Reading – Standards 1, 2, & 4)

👓 Identify new words that the characters say in the story that appeal to the five senses. Draw a model of eye, ear, and mouth and explain how the new words look and sound according to the five senses. (2-5, Reading – Standards 1, 2, & 4)

👀 Pick out 3-4 conversation quotes written in the text and explain what they mean. (2-5, Reading – Standards 1, 2, & 4)

👀 Create an interactive vocabulary list and game using Kahoot (www.Kahoot.com) and share it with the class. (2-5, Reading – Standard 4)

👀 Create a Venn Diagram comparing and contrasting the two characters' actions when they arrived to the hill in the story. Use words or pictures to describe how they are different and alike. (2-5, Reading – Standards 1 & 2)

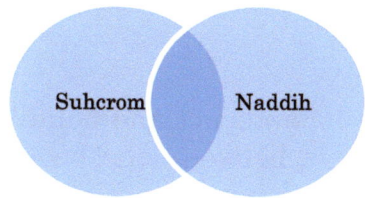

Writing Prompts

👀💡 Imagine that you are going on an adventure with your friends- when you find a skeleton or bones. Write a story about the adventure with illustrations. Publish the story and share it with the class. (2-5, Writing – Standards 3, 5, & 6)

👀💡 Create and share a Story Board using a mini-story board presentation board after reading and discussing the main ideas in chapters 4, 5 and 6. Include details that support the main ideas, use pictures and sentence strips to tell your story. (2-5, Writing – Standard 1)

👀💡 Use the language in the book to create your own language to express the feelings of the main characters as they make it to the hill. Write 3-4 lines of your new language to share. (2-5, Writing – Standard 1; 2-5, Speaking & Listening – Standard 1, 2, & 6)

 Draw and write a 5 page diary about the boys' adventures when they set up their tent, decided what supplies they would need and how they intended to collect those supplies. (2-5, Writing – Standard 1)

Create a conversation between the two characters based on what you know of their personalities and mannerisms. Use a 5-6 slide cartoon form paper that can be shared as a fold-out document (a long strip of paper divided into 5-6 squares that folds-out when you open it) with the class. (2-5, Writing – Standard 2)

Curriculum Connections

Boys or Nomads?
Watch a video clip to discover how nomads act and believe. Use a Venn Diagram to list three similarities and differences between the boys' identities as nomads and the boys' identities as boys going on adventures. How does the identity of a nomad and the identity of a boy going on an adventure change? (2-5, Reading – Standards 1 & 2)

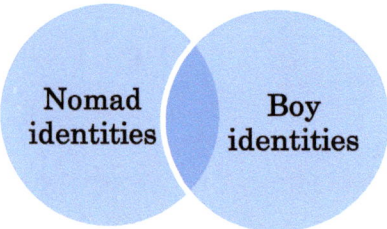

 Binocular Vision
Create binoculars out of toilet paper rolls and plastic wrap. Research how binoculars work. As you look into the binoculars think about what you have seen, heard, and read in the story so far. Discuss an idea that you have and how the binoculars are a symbol that symbolizes something from the story that you read so far. (2-5, Reading – Standards 1 & 2)

 **Desert Survival**

Discover what survival elements are important and what are not important to have in the desert. Do research about "wants" and "needs" based on what you may want on an adventure to what you may need on an adventure by creating a T-map of descriptive words. Then, share this with the class in a visual, digital presentation. (2-5, Reading – Standards 1, 2, and 6)

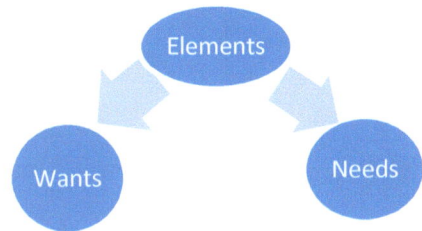

 Treasure Map

Find 5-6 pictures in old magazines or online of outdoor places including grass, trees, ocean, mountains, stones, rivers, and desserts. Use the pictures to create a treasure map. Cut the pictures out and paste them on a large piece of construction paper, number each picture as a clue and draw a treasure box at the end of the clues. Write the clues out on index cards. Have a partner follow your clues until he/she finds the treasure box. Follow your partner's clues on his/her treasure map. Explain to the class how your treasure map is like an adventure that Suhcrom and Naddih are going on. Explain that the treasure represents the new adventure that the characters are going on. (2-5, Reading – Standards 1 & 2)

 Plotting an Adventure

Research and develop an adventure plotting seven points of travel in a Nomad Adventure beginning at the bottom of the hill and ending at Suhcrom and Naddih's home. Use a timeline to extend your adventure with a POW-TOON at www.powtooons.com describing events you encountered along the way. (2-5, Reading – Standards 1 & 2)

 **Buddy Book**

Create a buddy book to share with your friends about: "If you could go follow the main characters anywhere, where would you go and who would you take with you? (2-5, Reading – Standards 1 & 2)

Research & Imagination Activities

 **Imagine Helmet...**

Imagine Helmet, a blind dog, visiting many places in the desert. Draw and color the animal. Tell how the boys might feel when seeing this blind dog before their adventure by creating captions for the pictures. Describe their feelings after reflecting on the bones that they find and the possibility that it could be Helmet. (2-5, Writing – Standards 2, 6, 7, & 8; 2-5, Reading – Standard 9)

 **Imagine Being a Nomad...**

Imagine you are playing with your friends pretending to be a Nomad and are out all day in the desert. Describe the experience by creating a short-10-15 line script for a skit on what you would do and explaining what you would find on your adventure. (2-5, Writing – Standards 2, 6, 7, & 8)

 **Imagine One Animal...**

Imagine that you could bring one animal (Camel, Sheep, or Dog) with you on an adventure in the desert. Which animal would you bring and why? Research more about the animal to support your choice. In a presentation to the class, dress up like the animal that you choose and state 3-5 facts you researched supporting why this would be the best animal to bring to the desert. (2-5, Writing – Standards 2, 6, 7, & 8; 2-5, Reading – Standard 9)

Silly Nomads From Palmerston Close - Volume 1

Lesson #2   Home Connection Activities

🏠 Find a pot and a pan and put them on a table in your house. Take 3-4 sheets of white copy paper and make different things to cook in your pot and pan on the white paper. Cut out the items and tell what you are cooking, and who you are cooking them for (Suhcrom or Naddih or both) and why.

🏠 Make a paper-doll figure out of tagboard (hard paper). Make this paper-doll stand up. Name this paper doll Jomfeh. According to what you have read so far about Jomfeh, imagine you are Suhcrom or Naddih and create a 2 minute conversation between you and the paper-doll.

🏠 Find a pillow at your house and lay down on it for a minute, pretend you just woke up from a wonderful Silly Nomad adventure. Tell a parent about this adventure and why it was so exciting. Draw and color a picture depicting part of the adventure.

🏠 Make 2-3 lightning bugs out of foil and put them in an old food jar. Take this jar and shake it - blink your eyes 5-6 times. Look at the lightning bugs and describe what they look like and sound like.

WE CONNECTED!

My favorite character in this part of the story was _____

because he/she_____

I liked the part in the story when _____

_____

I circled the house beside of the activity we completed.

Student: _____   Date:_____

Parent(s): _____   Date:_____

This page may be copied for student/parent use.

Silly Nomads From Palmerston Close

Lesson #3   Chapters 7-8   Pages 69-106

Lesson Focus: Suhcrom and Naddih experiment with a toilet, sweat through a pop-quiz, and dream of going to America. They plan their next adventure as ninjas rather than nomads.

Basic Story Vocabulary   (2-5, Reading – Standard 4)

pity	abruptly	plantains	ordeal
frolicked	interrogate	smirked	stutter
sweltering	churned	whimsically	oasis
recounted	brewing	inklings	fantasy
pensively	infamous	rapscallions	interject

Pre-teach vocabulary to introduce students to new words prior to reading the chapter. Choose an *Instructional Vocabulary Activity* from page 31.

Reading the Text

Silly Nomads books make fun read-aloud experiences for students. Varying these strategies reinforces interaction with text and creates ongoing interest for students. Choose a *Read-Aloud Strategy* from page 32-33 for in-class reading.

Facilitated Discussion Prompts

👀 Discuss in pairs for 2-3 minutes with what and how the boys made the new binoculars they would use on their next adventure. (2-5, Speaking & Listening – Standards 1, 2, & 6)

👀 Discuss with a group what kinds of things you would take on an adventure if you could only take (3) things including the binoculars. (2-5, Speaking & Listening – Standards 1, 2, & 6)

👀 Predict, discuss and make a strong inference about what will happen if their sister Enomih opens the bathroom door and finds them getting the supplies they need for the binoculars. (2-5, Speaking & Listening – Standards 1, 2, & 6)

👀 Listen to a short 1 to 2 minute YouTube audio presentation about Jamaican breakfast foods including plantains. Explain several different ways plantains may be made. (2-5, Speaking & Listening – Standards 1, 2, & 6)

👀 With a partner, tell a 2-3 minute story about an adventure that you might go on. Tell about the lunch that you would pack to take with you on this adventure. (2-5, Speaking & Listening – S plan standards 1, 2, & 6)

Reading Comprehension Activities

👀 Recount the sequence of events during the bathroom incident by creating a cartoon frame for each specific event. Place a star in the events you found to be the funniest. (2-5, Reading – Standard 2)

👀 How did the boys decide to be ninjas for their next adventure?
(2-5, Reading – Standards 1, 2, & 4)

👀 Identify new words that the characters say in the story such as "Camelfledge" and "cerasse tea"- that appeal to the five senses. Draw a model of eye, ear, and mouth and explain how the new words look and sound according to the five senses. (2-5, Reading – Standards 1, 2, & 4)

👀 What did you learn about Suhcrom from the pop quiz experience? (2-5, Reading – Standards 1 & 2)

👀 Create an interactive vocabulary list and game using Kahoot (www.Kahoot.com) and share it with the class. (2-5, Reading – Standard 4)

👀 Create a Venn Diagram comparing and contrasting how you believe the adventures of nomads and ninjas will be similar and different. Use words or pictures to describe how they are different and alike. (2-5, Reading – Standards 1 & 2)

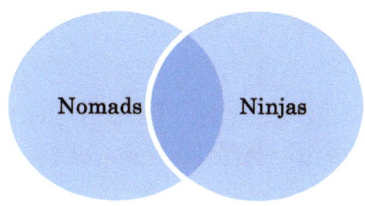

Writing Prompts

👀 💡 Imagine that you decide to continue the nomad adventure with one or two of your friends. Write the next adventure. (2-5, Writing – Standards 3, 5, & 6)

👀 💡 Have you ever experimented in the bathroom like the Nomads? How did your experience turn out? Write about your own experience. (2-5, Writing – Standard 1)

👀 💡 In this section, Suhcrom and Naddih dream of going to America. Write about a place you dream of visiting. (2-5, Writing – Standard 1)

 Draw the scene on page 95. Label each item in the scene and place in parenthesis whether it was pretend or real. (Ex.: fire – pretend).   (2-5, Writing – Standard 1)

 How did the boys know their Nomads adventure was over? Write an email from the boys to their father explaining why the Nomads adventure has ended and what they anticipate next.   (2-5, Writing – Standard 2)

Curriculum Connections

 **America & Jamaica**
Watch a video clip to discover more about the United States of America. Use a Venn Diagram to list three similarities and differences between the United States and Jamaica.   (2-5, Reading – Standards 1 & 2)

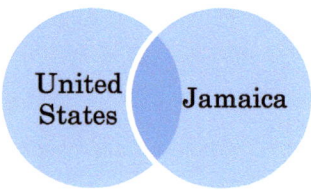

 **Jamaica Snack Tasting**
Discover the best way to make plantains. Describe the taste based on your research by creating a bubble map of descriptive words. Then, create your own plantain recipe. Type it up on a recipe card and try to make it with a parent.   (2-5, Reading – Standards 1, 2, and 6)

 **3-D Figure**
Create a 3-D figure symbolizing something from this part of the story. (2-5, Reading – Standards 1 & 2)

 **Travel Magic Carpet**

Make a magic carpet out of an old blanket or towel. Imagine you are going to take a trip from Jamaica to America. Who would go with you on your carpet? What stops would you make along the way? Create a map of your journey. (2-5, Reading – Standards 1 & 2)

 **Plotting an Adventure**

Research and develop a timeline plotting 7 points of travel in a Nomad Adventure beginning in a Jamaican city and ending in an American city. Use the timeline to extend your adventure to power point describing events you encountered along the way. (2-5, Reading – Standards 1 & 2)

 **Science of Toilet Workings**

The Silly Nomads experienced the scientific workings of a toilet when they worked quickly to plunge a toilet. Research how toilets work. Draw a visual image of how a toilet works, explain how the toilet clogged and why the plunger helped. (2-5, Reading – Standards 1 & 2)

Research & Imagination Activities

 **Imagine Waking Up …**

Imagine sleep walking and waking up in a new place that you are unfamiliar with. Luckily, you have a friend who will give you 5 good clues about where you are and what kind of adventure you will go on next. In pairs, take turns giving clues. Then guess where you are and what adventure you will go on. Next, give your friend a turn to do the same. (2-5, Writing – Standards 2, 6, 7, & 8; 2-5, Speaking & Listening – Standards 1, 2, & 6)

 **Inside a Tent...**

Imagine you are a Nomad inside a tent. Create a real tent by securing a 3 foot piece of rope (like a clothes line across an area) Put a blanket over the rope and secure the blanket with six heavy books. Climb inside the tent and listen to sounds that you have recorded earlier. Discuss what is making those sounds on the outside of your tent. Record 2-3 more sounds that you could be listening to while lying in your tent. (2-5, Speaking & Listening – Standards 1, 2, & 6)

 **Imagine Jamaica...**

Imagine living in Jamaica and going on an adventure with Suhcrom and Naddih as Ninjas. Research more about the country and their culture. Design and create a diorama of real adventures in Jamaica based on your findings. (2-5, Writing – Standards 2, 6, 7, & 8; 2-5, Reading – Standard 9)

 **Imagine Silly Nomads in America...**

Imagine a Silly Nomads adventure in America! Write and act out a Silly Nomads adventure in your own town with Suhcrom and Naddih. Research local landmarks and experiences they may have for the first time. Write a script, create props, and perform for the class. (2-5, Writing – Standards 2, 6, 7, & 8; 2-5, Reading- Standard 9)

Silly Nomads From Palmerston Close - Volume 1

Lesson #3   Home Connection Activities

🏠 Find 6 pages of construction paper and fold this to make a flip book of a twelve day Nomad adventure with Suhcrom and Naddih. On each of the pages, create a title of their location that day. Draw and color a picture of the adventure and staple the book's spine together when you are finished. Share this flipbook with your parent.

🏠 Create a 2-3 page skit of an adventure to America using at least 3 of the characters from the Silly Nomads book. Pick a place in Americia that the characters would travel to and tell about their adventure through the dialogue. Perform this skit in front of your parents.

🏠 Draw you favorite scene from this part of the book. Add a short paragraph explaining why this scene is your favorite.

🏠 Make a city map of a city in Americia that Suhcrom and Naddih will visit next, not as Nomads, but as Ninjas. Include who they would meet up with on the way and include any difficult situations that they may get into, as well as solutions.

WE CONNECTED!

My favorite character in this part of the story was _____

because he/she _____

I liked the part in the story when _____

_____

I circled the house beside of the activity we completed.

Student: _____   Date: _____

Parent(s): _____   Date: _____

This page may be copied for student/parent use.

Instructional Vocabulary Activities

(2-5, Reading – Standard 4)

Frayer Diagram: Divide the paper into fourths. Write a vocabulary word in the center (or the intersection of both lines). In one corner, place your own definition of the word. In the second corner, place facts or characteristics of the vocabulary word, and in the third, place examples of the word, and in the fourth, place non-examples of the word.
http://www.longwood.edu/staff/jonescd/projects/educ530/aboxley/graphicorg/fraym.htm

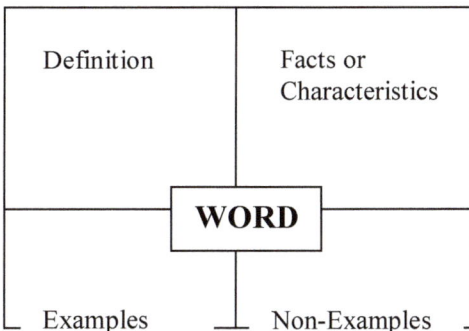

Word Sorts: Organize all of the vocabulary words into groupings that have common characteristics. Make up as many grouping titles as needed to go with the groupings. To vary the activity, sort the words by character association (which words are best associated with which story character), a great pre and post reading activity.

Add Words to an Interactive Word Wall: Include every new vocabulary word introduced on an interactive word wall. Interactive word walls are comprised of a wall or classroom space, wall, door, bulletin board, divider, etc. which is designated for these new words. Words are printed or created and then placed on the wall for frequent student use through discussion, writing, review, reading, grouping, illustration, or manipulation throughout classroom activities. The more the words are used following introduction, the more effective and interactive the Word Wall becomes for students.

Read-Aloud Strategies

(2-5, Speaking & Listening – Standards 1 & 2; 2-5, Reading – Standard 4)

Buddy Reading: Place students into pairs prior to reading. Students take turns reading out loud to each other, each a page or paragraph at a time.

Popcorn Reading (after Silent Pre-Reading): After an initial silent reading of the passage, one person begins to read the passage aloud. As soon as he/she stops reading, another student "pops" in to continue where the previous student stopped reading. It is helpful to set ground rules at the beginning of this activity, such as a maximum or minimum number of sentences or words read. This activity reinforces attention to print, listening, and collaboration as the object is to complete a passage in a smooth manner. It is important to allow the students to take the initiative to read rather than calling on them.

Jigsaw Reading: Jigsaw reading is helpful for use with longer passages or multiple passages of related text content. Split the passage(s) into sections and assign each section to a group of students so that every group reads a different part of the entire passage. The groups work together to read and understand their assigned passage. Their responsibility is to return to the whole group to summarize and/or teach them the content of their assigned passage. As a variation, allow the groups choices in how they teach the content to the entire group.

Choral Reading: Choral reading can be accomplished several different ways. It can include an initial silent read, and preplanning of how the passage can be most effectively read together. Choose parts of the passage to be read chorally, all students reading aloud together, and parts to be read aloud by one person or several different people. Commonly, the specific parts you want students to recall are those selected for choral reading. Choral reading can be fun as well as support and encourage listening skills and active engagement.

Read with Main Idea or Timeline Maps/Advanced Organizers: Main idea maps are a type of advanced organizer that effectively supports students in getting meaning from passages. A skeleton main idea map is most helpful in starting students with this strategy. Provide a web or diagram showing the main idea of the passage, as well as designated blank areas for the main points supporting the main idea that are connected to the main idea. Students read the passage aloud or silently and complete the map with the main points, as well as minor detail supporting those main points. This can be accomplished collectively out loud or as individuals in silence. In time, students can move to creating their own mind maps of passages. Use SmartArt in Microsoft Word for templates.

Oral Reading with CLOZE: For younger students, the teacher can read the book aloud to a group of students, periodically pausing for students to complete the appropriate word in text based on listening comprehension, syntax, and language skills.

Live Theatre Reading: After an initial reading of the passage, allow students to take different character roles within the story and read it as a play. The narrator reads any parts not in direct quotations. This interactive reading, especially when done in small groups, allows students to practice reading skills while they pay close attention to quotation marks, conversation between characters, and listening skills.

ASSESSMENTS

Pre and Post Assessments, Quizzes, and
Reading Comprehension Assessments
may be copied for student use.

Silly Nomads From Palmerston Close - Volume 1
Pre and Post Assessment

Place T (truth) or M (myth) by each statement.

Pre	Statement	Post
	An imaginary adventure can seem real even if it is not.	
	Jamaica is a wealthy country.	
	Creating things with what you have is as good as buying the real item.	
	Nomads wander around the desert with camels and sheep.	
	Construction sites make good playgrounds.	
	Documentaries are more entertaining than informational.	
	The sun can help you tell time.	
	Desert survival requires preparation.	
	You can be fond of a tradition even if you don't like it.	
	People from other countries often view America as a country much like their own.	
	An oasis in the desert is not a good place to set up camp.	
	Crabs are easier to catch at night than in the daytime.	

Silly Nomads From Palmerston Close - Volume 1
Pre and Post Assessment

Answer Key

Pre	Statement	Post
T	An imaginary adventure can seem real even if it is not.	
M	Jamaica is a wealthy country.	
T	Creating things with what you have is as good as buying the real item.	
T	Nomads wander around the desert with camels and sheep.	
M	Construction sites make good playgrounds.	
M	Documentaries are more entertaining than informational.	
T	The sun can help you tell time.	
T	Desert survival requires preparation.	
T	You can be fond of a tradition even if you don't like it.	
M	People from other countries often view America as a country much like their own.	
M	An oasis in the desert is not a good place to set up camp.	
T	Crabs are easier to catch at night than in the daytime.	

Silly Nomads From Palmerston Close - Volume 1

Lesson #1 Quiz   Chapters 1-3

1. How did Naddih get Suhcrom to wake up and join him in the beginning of the story?
   a. Naddih gave Suhcrom tea
   b. Naddih made a rooster sound
   c. Naddih reminded Suhcrom of the plans they made several days earlier and Suhcrom remembered this.

2. In the documentary that Naddih and Suhcrom watched, what language was spoken by the nomads?
   a. Arabic
   b. Spanish
   c. Egyptian

3. In a paragraph, describe the neighborhood called "Palmerston Close".

4. Which supplies did Naddih and Suhcrom NOT have when they met at their secret location with their friends?
   a. apples
   b. crocus bag
   c. oil lamp

5. According to the story, how can the area where the characters live be described?
   a. an area of giant mansions
   b. small friendly village
   c. big city with skyscrapers

6. Which character wanted to tell Sterlin and Rodney about the Nomad adventure?
   a. Suhcrom
   b. Naddih
   c. Hamburg

7. When Rodney says "Luk ova desso man, shine di light ova desso", what did he mean?
   a. He caught the crab
   b. That he and the boys should go home
   c. He thinks he sees the crab moving by him

8. Which statement describes the boys' reaction to the crab?
   a. It's smaller than a sea shell!
   b. What a beautiful color!
   c. Wow! That is the biggest thing we've ever laid eyes on!

9. What did the boys say when they were trying to catch the crab?
   a. This crab is bigger than Sterlin's dog.
   b. This crab is smaller than Sterlin's cat.
   c. This crab is bigger than Sterlin's cat.

10. Why did Naddih and Suhcrom NOT want to tell the other boys about their coming Nomad adventure?
    a. They thought the boys would copy what they were doing.
    b. They knew the boys would tell everyone and everyone would laugh at them.
    c. They thought the other boys did not deserve to go on their special adventure.

Silly Nomads From Palmerston Close - Volume 1

Lesson #2 Quiz   Chapters 4-6

1. As Suhcrom and Naddih began their adventure on the hill, they estimated the time to be ten o'clock because of the
    a. position of the sun
    b. position of the moon
    c. position of the tent

2. When Suhcrom and Naddih first found the bones/skeleton, they initially thought that the bones were
    a. an animal
    b. Helmet
    c. a Nomad

3. What things did Naddih NOT guess could have happened before they became bones?
    a. bitten by a snake
    b. eaten by a wild animal
    c. drown by an alligator

4. Why did Naddih's lip quiver when he discussed the bones?
    a. he was afraid of thinking about it
    b. he was happy it was not him
    c. he thought about how hungry he was

5. How did Suhcrom try to mess with Naddih's mind?
    a. he talked about Malaria
    b. he talked about Gangrene
    c. he talked about the mosquito

6. According to the text, Helmet is BOTH a
   a. food and a disease
   b. game and a dog
   c. activity and adventure

7. Suhcrom teased Naddih and said that they fed the dog Helmet
   a. festival and sprat fish
   b. figurative and spoke fish
   c. favorite and spot fish

8. When you blindfold someone and turn them around and around you can find out what it is like to
   a. be hungry and sleepy
   b. be blind and dizzy
   c. be happy and silly

9. According to the documentary that Suhcrom and Naddih always watched on TV, the best animal to bring with you to the desert is
   a. A camel
   b. A dog
   c. A rat

10. Why did Naddih mark an X in the sand when talking to Suhcrom?
    a. To explain where the next oasis would be
    b. To explain how to get home
    c. To mess with Suhcrom

Silly Nomads From Palmerston Close - Volume 1

Lesson #3 Quiz   Chapters 7-8

1. Suhcrom and Naddih thought they would get in trouble if Enomih knew about them
    a. Clogging up the toilet
    b. Making binoculars
    c. Being late for dinner

2. Suhcrom and Naddih were brothers that
    a. Counted on each other
    b. Did not get along
    c. Were twins

3. Who in the book had a speech impediment according to him?
    a. Enomih
    b. Suhcrom
    c. Naddih

4. Suhcrom figured out in the last chapter that Naddih was
    a. the shoelace bandit
    b. a serious boy
    c. the Ninja

5. While drinking the cerasse tea
    a. Suhcrom thought Naddih was delirious
    b. Naddih thought Suhcrom was delirious
    c. Both Suhcrom and Naddih were delirious

6. What superhero did Suhcrom want to be first?
   a. Captain America
   b. Superman
   c. Tarzan

7. Why did both boys NOT want to be the Joker?
   a. because he is evil
   b. because he is smart
   c. because he is not popular

8. *All the sidewalks are littered with candy and million dollar bills.*
   The boys are talking about...
   a. America
   b. Palmerston Close
   c. Jamaica

9. Suddenly the gale wind...
   a. ripped the tent right out from underneath them
   b. blew through the town uprooting flowers
   c. made a gigantic noise that scared both the boys

10. At the end of the Nomad adventure the boys decided to be
    a. Senior Nomads
    b. Silly Nomads
    c. Silly Ninjas

Silly Nomads From Palmerston Close - Volume 1

Quiz Answer Key

Question	Lesson 1 Quiz	Lesson 2 Quiz	Lesson 3 Quiz
1	C	A	A
2	A	C	A
3	*	C	C
4	A	A	A
5	B	A	A
6	B	B	B
7	C	A	A
8	C	B	A
9	C	A	A
10	B	A	C

*The neighborhood was a small residential neighborhood within the town of Portsmouth on the island of Jamaica. Answers may vary: small neighborhood in Jamaica, in a small town, on an island, in Jamaica called Palmerston Close.

Silly Nomads From Palmerston Close - Volume 1

Reading Comprehension Assessment

1. Compare and contrast the lives of Suhcrom and Naddih with the lives of real nomads. Use a Venn Diagram or a T-chart to share your thoughts.

2. Do your parents view education the same way Jomfeh does? Give an example that shows how your parents feel about education.

3. How do you think Suhcrom and Naddih would explain to someone how to use their imagination?

4. Give 1 example of the power of imagination in the story.

5. Which character in the story is most like you? Explain why.

Silly Nomads®

Look for these other Silly Nomads adventures!

Volume 2 – Silly Nomads Go Ninja Crazy

Volume 3 – Silly Nomads Jubilee Bike Race Heroes

Volume 4 – Coming Soon

www.ingramcontent.com/pod-product-compliance
Lightning Source LLC
Chambersburg PA
CBHW060810010526
44116CB00002B/35